ADDRESS

ON

The Duty of the Slave States

IN THE PRESENT CRISIS,

Delivered in Galveston, Dec. 12th, 1860

BY REV. J. E. CARNES,

By special invitation of the Committee of Safety and Correspondence, and many of the oldest citizens.

GALVESTON:
Printed at the "News" Book and Job Office.
1860.

ADDRESS,

ON

The Duty of the Slave States

IN THE PRESENT CRISIS.

By Rev. J. E. CARNES.

DELIVERED IN GALVESTON, DECEMBER 12, 1860, BY SPECIAL INVITATION OF THE COMMITTEE OF SAFETY AND CORRESPONDENCE, AND MANY OF THE OLDEST CITIZENS.

Ladies and Gentlemen:

Let any one who is prompt to regard my position at this moment as extraordinary, not forget that the present is an extraordinary time, and that, having no precedent to guide me, I have been compelled to make such response to the invitation to address you as my own judgment might suggest. No one, therefore, is responsible but myself. The Church to which I have the honor to belong, is not a political body, and has no politics—none whatever. In ecclesiastical matters she speaks for herself through her own accredited organs. But in civil affairs she has no voice, and wants none. So that when one of her members exercises any strictly civil right, he does so as a citizen without acknowledging her authority, or wishing to be understood as acting in anywise on her behalf. In becoming a minister of religion at her altar, I simply pledged myself to do nothing which might reasonably be expected to reflect injury upon that office. My address to-night will not do so: the God of the Bible is the Lord of nations, and every crisis in their history is but a revelation of His Providence. I am not afraid to speak, here or elsewhere, what I believe to be the teachings of that Providence. But no one can see all sides at once; I give what appears to be the truth from my own point of view.

Before proceeding to do so, let me state the issue. It has been done for me in a late speech by Judge Roberts of our Supreme Court:

"The great question before the American people is : shall the institution of slavery be put upon a sure basis of gradual extinction. The Northern controlling majorities say it shall. The South say it shall not. And that is the issue."

The man who would dispute that statement of the question is so far behind the times that it would take all night to get back to him. I proceed: in the same speech it is shown that the measures adopted at the North for the extinction of slavery have now gained advantages which "cannot be successfully opposed, or averted, except by prompt State action, and that we are justified in pursuing that remedy to any extent that may be necessary to secure our endangered rights." After showing that a State Convention may be called, with or without the sanction of the State authorities, Judge Roberts teaches that "it may declare the people absolved from their fealty to the General Government." He further says:

"The remedy itself (that is, secession) may be adopted conditionally, for the purpose of placing the State on equal terms in treating for an adjustment of satisfactory guarantees against future violations of its rights, or absolutely for the purpose of final separation."

This I regard as very important, because it affords a "platform" upon which all can unite. Those who think "something should be done," can here find a decided position—leaving time and the progress of events to determine whether they will demand "final separation" or yield to such proposals for continuing the Union as the North may choose to make. Any less decided ground than this, I regard as very unsafe at the present time. As to the fears of precipitation which may be entertained by some, I cannot better express myself than in the noble, generous and just words of Judge Roberts:

"I have no fears that inconsiderate rashness will control them. They have pondered upon the issues of this crisis long and well. It is not unexpected. They have their minds made up about it. There is no agrarian spirit in this country. There is no war of classes. There is no conflict between labor and capital. Our people are not asking or seeking to extort any favors from the government to themselves, or deprive others of any rights. They have no motive or desire for a social rupture at home. Their excitement arises from an entirely opposite cause—a high resolve now to throw themselves into the breach, not to destroy but to protect rights; not to destroy property, but to protect property; not to destroy life, but to make life worth having; not to produce discord, but to end it. Their excitement is not a shallow, noisy riffle, but a deep irresistible current, founded on the firmest conviction of the mind. I do not distrust the people of my State. I will not yield to any argument founded on their want of discretion, want of intelligence, want of integrity to act for themselves, in a serious emergency, and to act now upon it."

And now, fellow-citizens, I give my own solemnly entertained opinion as to "the duty of the Southern States in the present crisis." These are the words of my invitation to address you: my reply—given of course under a full conviction of the weakness of human judgment—is, that the Southern States should now "strike, and firmly, and one stroke," and let that stroke be SECESSION FROM THE FEDERAL UNION!

But, it is said, we have friends at the North—shall we desert them? Fellow-citizens, the best of those friends have long predicted that we would be forced to secession, and our continuance in the Union will be to give up; on our part, the spirit of independence and self-respect, which made those Northern men our friends. The colonies had friends in Great Britain—some of the most influential and high-spirited men of the realm—who predicted the revolution as a result of the policy of aggression. Had not the colonies seceded, those men would have been found false witnesses of freedom herself, or of the minds "nourished in the wild,"

> "—— Where nursing Nature smiled
> On infant Washington."

It is due to our truest Northern friends that we secede. They are begging us to relieve them of the burden of their helpless struggle against fanaticism. Others seem to be faintly hoping that "something may be done;" and still others—that large class which believe that slavery is an evil to be tolerated only according to contract—are melting away in the fierce glare of abolitionism, like snow before the flame. When it waxeth warm, they vanish; what time it is hot they are consumed out of their places. The utterances of the Plymouth pulpit are very good specimens of the preponderant Northern sentiment. Here is a quotation from a report of a late thanksgiving discourse:

"He counseled forbearance, indulgence, respect for the rights of the several States. He spoke eloquently and kindly of the South. Our interests in commercial and manufactures were coincident. We shared a common historic glory. We can feel toward them no envy nor jealousy. We must stand by the original bond—by the Constitution. We will earnestly fulfill every duty to the South, and we will do no more, though the heavens fall, though States unclasp their hands, and the Union is severed."

This sounds liberal; but let me read again from the same sermon:

"On the question before the country we must take sides. Which should we take? If we take the north side, we go for civilization; if we take the south side, we go for barbarism. There were good people at the South. He spoke of institutions, and insisted that those of the North were on the side of civilization and those of the South on the side of barbarism. The prevailing conflict was a conflict between civilization and barbarism. The South and the North in the early days of the Republic found engrafted upon them the poisonous colonial seeds of slavery.—The North abandoned the institution, the South cherished it. We now reap a harvest of peace, the South reaps a harvest of tumults and agitations. They expect to be as well off with their curse, as we are without it. They are not, and they expect us to make it up to them. For this reason our government has been forced into a false position and placed in the character of an unjust judge. The Southern States are founded on a system of society rotten at the core ; the North has a vital heart. The two systems are in conflict. One or the other must yield. Either liberty must give way, or oppression succumb."

Another speaker, the Rev. Dr. Bellows, of New York, who always speaks kindly of the South, and has not a fibre of the mere fanatic in his composition, bore this testimony on the same day: (Nov. 29, 1860.)

"The speaker then adverted to the growth of the anti-slavery sentiment in the North, and maintained that the natural repugnance to that institution was inevitable and irresistible. This confederacy, henceforth, was to be governed in the interests of freedom. The North could not alter her moral code, nor lay aside her deliberate convictions or abolish her popular majorities. The free States cannot take a step backwards."

This is a fair sample of "the larger portion of northern friendship for the south and from such friendship we must effect a speedy deliverance before it proves our ruin. Our commercial friends at the North will be as much our friends after secession, as they were before.

But it is asked, Will not secession deepen the conflicts of the border ? I think it will be the best peace measure we can adopt. Suppose the Northern States were slaveholding : there would then be a "free country" along their Northern borders. Would there be border difficulties with Canada ? There would not and why ? Because religion, and phylosophy, morality and all other good things, combine to make people living under different governments, let each other alone. It is much easier then, for each to say, "we have nothing to do with the matter," so far as the interests of the other are concerned, than where they are bound together under the same Constitution, and subjected to the agitations of popular elections. Give the North slaves ; annex Canada, then the struggle for the control of the Government commences, and then commences also, the growths of fanaticism, sectional hates and border warfares, rank, deadly and irrepressible.

Break up the struggle for the power of the Federal Government, and you will give such peace and security to the border as it never can enjoy while that conflict lasts, and last it will, under the present rate of things, forever, or until slavery is exterminated.

But, suppose the Northern States were to repeal their Personal Liberty Bills, and give bonds to keep the peace, either by pledges or by an amendment of the Constitution, would you then be willing to give up the idea of secession ? For myself, I answer, unequivocally, I would not. Were the North now to grant us everything we might ask, there would be a large minority there opposed to it, which would, in a few years, become the majority on that very question as an issue. By that time, the South would be powerless to resist, or to secede. Now, I think, is the tide in her affairs, which if not taken at the flood will leave her hopelessly astrand. We are not now that strength which we were in old days when we commenced to concede and compromise ; but, I trust it can be added—

> " ——that which we are, we are ;
> One equal temper of heroic hearts,
> Made weak by time and fate, but strong in will
> To strive, to seek, to find—no more to yield."

I turn from these topics to others, of which these are, probably, but the indicators. We seem to be brought face to face with a revelation of Providence in history. Government and nationality are among the most potent means which God has chosen for the moral and religious elevation of mankind. He it is that appoints nations their " bounds of habitation," to the end that they may feel after Him and find Him. These are His own words; and wherever a people are called to deliberate upon the formation of an independent government, they deal with principles as sacred as morality and religion can make them.

God has three great records : the book of inspiration, the book of nature, and the book of history. They all agree. But thefirst named is the key to the others. I have just now quoted a passage which proclaims separate nationalities to be among the means of moral elevation. ature and history concur—the one with her differences of surface and climate produces the varieties of the "one blood" which are necessary to separate governments, and the other holds up her record of events to show that judicious separations of men into independent nationalities is the necessary law of human progress. I say " separations," because addition comes before division. Looking backward to antiquity you see vast aggregations of men. These were not nations, but the material out of which nations were to be made. Before the birth of sciences and ideas, men were overwhelmed by the vastness of material nature, and huddled together in swarms. It was the sentiment of fear which gathered them on the plains of Shinar to build the Tower of Babel ; and ever since, that same sentiment of fear has been causing them to unite for some similar impossible end of safety. God then visited them with confusion of speech, which must have involved differences in the method of arriving at truth as well as in the sounds and signs by which it is expressed. Ideas are, indeed, the basis of nationalities. Every one must agree with the philosophy which declares that no nation which has not an idea to work out has any excuse for its existence. Has the world gone backward ? No sane man can believe it. If it has gone forward, most certainly it has progressed from the epoch of chaotic agglomeration to the epoch of harmonious diversity. This at least is the tendency. It is the true spirit of the age. The nations, if such they can be called, which are at the greatest distance from it are the most barbarous. What is the condition of the dissolution of the Chinese and Russian empires ? The progress of enlightenment. Who believes that England can retain her vast colonial possessions any longer than the moment when they first begin to think ? No sooner did the revolutionary fathers get adjusted to their new position and begin to cast their eyes about them, than the question of separation from England began to be agitated. It mattered not that she was the mother country; and that the lands of the new people were held in her name—that she had human law, associations and powers on her side ; the colonies had the law of Providence on theirs—the law that "the element of division is the condition of history." Nor can any sentiment call back, or any power check the flow of historical development. Ever and anon secession has become a necessity, from the days of Abraham to the days of Washington and Garibaldi. Nor will it ever cease to become a necessity so long as the law of growth prevails. My own impression is that two or more nations were born at once on the 4th of July 1776, and that the Constitution was the nurse appointed to take care of them until they became able to take care of themselves. The Constitution was not their mother ; they were born of history ; and they inherit her instinct of division. It has been manifesting itself through all the period of their childhood, and has now taken possession of their reason, and their conscience, and will never rest until it has been embodied in act. Their reluctant acceptance of the Union was the first prophecy of its dissolution, and all the events since that time have been conspiring to the fulfillment of that prophecy. The present appeal of the Constitution to the South is much like Pharaoh's daughter might have been to Moses : "I found you floating a helpless thing upon the Nile, and have protected you until you are grown to manhood and to greatness." "Nevertheless," the conduct of the Israelitish law giver seemed to say, "I am not your son." He had "come to years." So the South, grown out of her minority, refuses to be called the daughter of the Constitution. She knows better. She feels it in her bones. Long as she has been to school in the house of the Constitution, she has not forgotten her mother ; and when the old lady comes to the door and calls, the voice of nature asserts its supremacy. The daughter was loaned, not given, to the schoolmaster ; she will go where she belongs.

The argument that we have done well under the Constitution is fallacious. It is just the same as to say that because a boy has done well as an apprentice, he should never be a boss. The change from infancy to manhood may be very gradual and delightful ; but that will hardly avail to keep one forever within the bounds of irresponsible progress. See, what a change! At first the North was in favor of the slave trade because it provided employment for her ships, while the South was opposed to it because she had no employment for the slaves. Just then commenced what the historians call "an astonishing career of discovery." Hargraves with his Jenny is followed by Arkwright with his spinning frame, and Cartwright with his loom, and Whitney with his gin, and Watt with his steam-engine. Nothing like this series of discoveries is known in the history of science. Millions are dependent upon them for bread, and hundreds of millions for comfort. Previously to 1790 the United States did not export a pound of cotton; in 1792 we exported 138,328 pounds; sixty years ago we exported about nineteen millions of pounds; now we export a billion of pounds and ten times nineteen millions for good measure. Seventy years ago the export value of cotton was nothing; now it is about two hundred millions of dollars. Such has been the expansion of an interest, the dim, unrevealed progress of which, was like to prove fatal to the formation of the Union. Underneath this expansion a marked change of moral sentiment has been going on, in order that when our material interest required division, the interests of morality might second the demand. At first the North cared but little about the moral principle involved, while at the South, there was a general thoughtfulness on that subject. The North was then more proslavery than the South. Each has changed, and the change has been necessary in both instances. It has been made with a view to the working out of the idea assigned to each.—The North has to work out the problem of the hirer and the hired; the South the problem of the owner and the owned. That both can be solved on christian principles and on christian principles alone, I profoundly believe. That the problems are akin, and that the progressive solution of the one will help towards the progressive solution of the other, is doubtless true. But to that end they must be separated. The solution is not to be intellectual, merely, but moral, and for that reason the moral responsibility of each must be thrown upon itself. Where does God plant the moral power when he makes a moral agent? In his own will. The State is also a moral agent, and must differ with itself only on questions of policy, never upon the question of morality. That is the foundation, and if it be destroyed what can the righteous do? Even England could not get along with the two problems of free and slave labor under the same government. And yet England and these Southern States could easily agree in a policy beneficial to each. Does any one suggest that our agreement would be conditioned on the waters that separate us? Did not wide waters separate the English isle from her slaveholding colonies? And yet she abolished slavery there, against the will of the masters, just as the North will abolish it here in spite of our protestations, unless we do what the English slaveholding colonies could or would not do—set up an independent government. As matters now stand Northern operatives and employers, instead of adjusting their own relations, join in demonstrations against the South, and the South, in turn, complains that these unjust and ignorant attacks upon her social system prevent her from discharging her full duty to the slave. God has given the South some millions of slaves to christianize; and before they have learned the duty of obedience, the North stirs them to rebellion with notions of liberty, and then laughs at the South for attempting to make anything presentable out of such an institution. Why? Underneath the whole agitation lies a false idea of moral responsibility. And this is fostered by holding the North to a connection with slavery, until in her distress to shake it off she nullifies the Federal Compact by the action of her State Legislatures, and violates sacred and essential usage in the election of a Presidential ticket of her own—a ticket for which no Southern State could have cast an electoral vote without incurring everlasting disgrace. And yet it is proposed to submit to the inauguration of such an administration in all the States of the South ? On the day when that is done the spirit of the South is broken forever. "If the salt have lost its savor wherewith shall it be salted ?—it is thenceforth fit for nothing but to be cast out and trodden under foot of man." A wise man assures us that the blessing of Judah and Issachar will never meet—no people can be at once the lion's whelp and the ass between burdens. It would seem that Providence, in order to drive us to secession, has removed from our position in the Union every plea but that of absolute vassalage. Let us not make ourselves ashamed to walk the soil of the South, while we live, and ashamed to lie down beneath it when we die!

There is no need, however, to trouble ourselves with imaginary evils. The South will not submit. As I have before intimated, we are just a commencement of the epoch of disintegration. Europe is struggling to break the chains of old alliances, and to adjust her nationalities according to their true relationships. Our peaceable division will do more to prevent bloodshed in these inevitable separations, than all other causes combined. Those who think our continued Union necessary to the force of our example, may be greatly mistaken. Suppose we form two separate governments without striking a blow, what greater triumph of Christian civilization could be exhibited ? It would be as much more influential for good, than the continuance of the Union could be, as it is more in accordance with the spirit of history, and the requirements of the age. Peace hath her victories no less renowned than war. Secession would be a revolution without anarchy, and without the shedding of a drop of blood. The example would rise on the world as the dawn of a new era in human affairs. Nothing contributes more to the perpetuation of war than the old condition of its necessity—that nothing can be done without it. Hitherto we have thought secession impossible without war, and some have been doing their best to think so still. But the rapid progress of events toward it, has thrown the ray of peace upon every dark cloud of the imagination. The old fighting impulse wakes up, and, with the instinct of courage, sees that there is nothing for it to do, and lies down to sleep again. No : the revolution is to be wholly a moral one, and it is as inevitable as it is moral. Let us see further why I think so.

When, just about one year ago, Mr. Charles O'Conor, delivered his opinion at the Union meeting in New York, that the Union must be abandoned, or that public sentiment at the North must turn away from political leaders who talk of negro slavery being an evil—or a bad bargain which must be tolerated only as a bad bargain—and come fully over to the ground that slavery was "just, benign, lawful and proper," everybody at the South felt the force and truth of that position. But Northern sentiment never can be brought to that state. There is one thing that could do it, and one alone, and that is the establishment of slavery in the Northern States. No moral idea can survive where there are no corresponding external facts to sustain it. The Southern people themselves could not believe in the justice, benignity and propriety of slavery, if they did not come in daily contact with it. If it did not interweave itself with their domestic relations; if they were not bound to it by the duties and sympathies growing out of the relation of master and servant;—if, in a word, it did not touch the heart it could never do much with the mind. Our servants must play with our children; we must bear them in our arms, ere yet the wool has lost its early brown; we must lean over their sick couches, and receive in turn the anodyne or the new position on the bed of pain from their hands, in order that feelings inexpressible as they are deep and tender may stir the heart—

"Then old missus, she feel mighty sad,
And de tears run down like de rain,
And then old massa, he feel very bad,
'Case he never see old Ned again."

Sow the doctrine that slavery is a good broadcast over the mind of a people which has no immediate connection with slavery, as often as you may, it will never take root. It is sown by the wayside and on stony ground, and will always be picked up by the birds of excitement. Nay, even admit the ground to be good of its kind, the harvest you expect to reap from it by such a process, will never do more than aggravate the terrors of the famine. Experience has shown that the people of the North are hostile to the negro and to slavery; reason teaches us that they must continue to be so; and the plainest dictates of honor and of safety agree in requiring us to rid them of the federal responsibility for its existence. Mr. O'Conor speaks of philosophy. There are various schools of philosophy. Mr. Seward's great power over the Northern masses springs from his philosophy. His teachings of the "irrepressible conflict," of "a ballot for every man or a bullet for every man," are good for the North, but he mingles them too easily with the declaration that the North is compelled to maintain the army and navy for the support of slavery, for Northern comfort, or for the interest of truth. The "irrepressible conflict" exists between labor and capital, and it is only the connection of the North with the South which turns it into the channels of national and congressional elections, to our continued annoyance and injury. His maxim "a bullet for every man or a ballot for every man," is very just in a free society where the laborer has to bear the responsibilities of a citizen. It is quite comfortable doubtless, for the Northern capitalist to pay his operative a few shillings for his week's labor, telling him to be sure to come by the polls on Monday morning and vote for the strong anti-slavery candidate. One of the strongest abolitionists I have ever seen in the North, was a seamstress who was scolded rudely out of a Jew store, because she was five minutes behind the hour with the garment, which she had made for a price so infinitesimal that, with the best intentions, I have not been able to retain it in my memory. Of such mothers abolitionists are born. They do not like slave labor—thank God !—and, therefore, keep away from the South. But I do not see why, with this thankfulness to escape the pleasure of their intimate acquaintance, we should continue to pay high prices to enable them to vote against us.

I recapitulate before proceeding to another topic. Separations are the law in modern history, as aggregations were in ancient. Smaller governments, the enlargement of international law, the greater importance of treaties, Congresses of nations, are to be the fruits of the general improvement of mankind. The years are just before us when no vast government will be possible. It is false to the teachings of a sound political philosophy to suppose that one great Republic can be built up and sustained on this continent. Old ideas of national glory, of star-spangled banners, and Yankee Doodles may have some hold upon our memories ; but we must have something better to live on than such classics as these. Each age has its problem. Men try to get rid of thought and responsibility. But they cannot evade these without incurring penalties and chastisements greater than they can bear.

While a great Federal Union lasts, there will always be a struggle for power, which will always be directed against the Slave States. There was no anti-slavery interest in the first Senate ; now a large slave interest is in the minority there ; and the late election shows that the North is determined not to let us have even the Vice President. We are in the minority of more than fifty in the Lower House. Half a dozen more States, all free, are knocking for admission. Wherever the carcass is, there the eagles will be gathered together. As fast as they are admitted, they will swell the ranks of the party whose one idea is the extirpation of slavery. Shall we still persist in the idea of a great Union ? On the contrary, we must turn this swelling Northern tide into different channels. If we form a Southern Republic, our example will be followed. The Northern States will separate into different governments. A corrupt and corrupting centralism will be abolished ; the resources of the continent will be developed, the character of the people elevated, and government, stripped of its gewgaws and cured of its idle fancies, will be put to work on the true principle of a division of labor. Each Republic, with a complete working system of its own, will be able to keep its government within bounds, under the supervision of the people ; and the inter-Republican meetings, which may from time to time be necessary for the regulation of matters pertaining to the general interest, will be conducted on higher principles than those which rule in our present Federal Legislature.

At first sight, the idea of "the balance of the power" disconcerts us by bringing the struggles of Europe to our minds. We need not console ourselves, however, with the notion that we are far ahead of all the rest of the world in the science of politics. If we have supposed that one huge government, republican in form, could develop and protect all the interests of this continent, we have concealed from ourselves the obvious truth that no written constitution can embrace different degrees of moral and intellectual progress, or solve all the problems of latitude and diversity of race. It were vain for the student of politics to look for satisfactory guidance on this subject to the writings and speeches of the early period of our history, whatever wisdom they may exhibit on other themes. Nor will the "great expounder" or the "great commoner" guide us beyond the immediately practical questions of their day. Webster and Clay saw only the pageantry of our politics. Both believed that our system would at some time be made consistent with itself by the extinction of slavery.—Calhoun alone of the great triumvirate saw the impossibility of this, and was driven by it to profound thought upon government in its original principles. Forced, as we are, to regard him as the representative statesman of the South, how pleasant it is to know that his life was as pure as his intellect was grand! This reflection will cheer every one who opens his "Disquisition on Government" and his "Discourse on the Constitution of the United States," and induce the hope of finding there some of those guiding principles which light the conclusions of the intellect only as they are furnished with the pure oil of the earnest, well-intentioned heart. Calhoun alone, of the statesmen of his day, wrote for posterity, leaving, to use his own language, "truth, plainly announced, to battle its own way." He alone foresaw this crisis in our history. His remedy was, the election of two Presidents, believing, as he did, that each section would strive to elect the man least obnoxious to the other, and that each section, being thus placed in possession of a negative or checking power upon the other, would endeavor so to shape its policy as to offer no obstruction to the working of the government. This remedy is the only one that can be applied with any hope of success, and it is in the belief that it will not be tried that I found my conviction of the present inevitability of disunion. Indeed, it may be doubted whether this remedy, although it be so plausible, does not itself suggest the propriety of two governments. However that may be, we must now believe with Mr. Calhoun that, "The end of the contest between separate interests, (under the same Constitution,) will be the subversion of the Constitution, either by the undermining process of construction—where its meaning will admit of possible doubt,—or by substituting what is called party-usage in place of its provisions;—or, finally, when no other contrivance would subserve the purpose, by openly and boldly setting them asside." The division between numerical or popular majorities, and concurrent majorities, or the voice of interests, is fundamental to the Constitution. The House of Representatives is the embodiment of the numerical majority, the Senate of the concurrent. Each has a negative upon the action of the other. So it is throughout, except with regard to the Presidency. The framers of the Constitution endeavored to guard this point also, as well as they could; but electoral colleges, choice by the House of Representatives, and all the other complications, have failed to prevent popular parties from attemping to secure and control the executive department. It is clear that the crisis was sure to come, as it has come, on the election of a President. And it seems evident that no compromise or guarantees can prevent its recurence. By the next time, the popular majority may have grown sufficiently bold to attempt the coersion of the South. A fair conclusion, on a view of the whole subject, is that a Constitution like ours is potent to regulate differences of power, but not to secure the rights of diverse interests—admirable in its efficiency to protect Vermont against Pennsylvania or New York, but wholly unable to defend the interests of slave States against the popular majorities of the North. Conflict seems certain unless disunion arrest present tendencies. For that we seem to be fully prepared, in the spirit of our people, which shrinks from the thought of the exercise of power over them by the President elect as from the touch of the leprosy—prepared in the consciousness of the Northern States that they are the aggressors—and prepared by the possession of the glorious old sheet-anchor of the state sovereignty which will prevent us from drifting into anarchy during the progress of separation and reconstruction.

The commercial crisis! Liberty has her crises as well as commerce. The outer courts have their interests; but there is a glory which must not depart from the shrine. Better for a people to break all images a thousand times, than permit freedom once to say—"they are joined to their idols, let them alone." Better that a crisis drive down the price of cotton than that it should sink the free spirit of a people. Commercial prosperity has risen refreshed from many a depression; but—

> "In vain might Liberty invoke
> The spirit to its bondage broke,
> Or raise the neck that courts the yoke."

The case of the South and the Union re minds me of King Arthur and Sir Bedivere. When the King at Lyonness knew that his hour had come, that the old must give place to the new, he told the Knight to take his sword Excalibur, and fling him into the middle of the lake. At first the Knight refused; he was too loyal to leave the King alone. At last, however he prevailed on himself to make a feint to do the bidding. But when he came to the margin of the meer, and drew forth the brand, and saw that the haft was rich with diamond studs and subtlest jewelry, it seemed better to him to leave Excalibur concealed among the withered water-flags upon the shore. His lust of gold betrayed itself to the King, and again the Knight was sent back. This time, he grew sentimental, and thought that with Excalibur much honor, reverence and fame were lost. The King pierced the cloud of this conceit also, and sent him back the third time, saying—

> "Thou wouldst betray me for the precious hilt,
> Either from lust of gold—or like a girl
> Valuing the giddy pleasure of the eyes.
> But if thou spare to fling Excalibur,
> I will arise and slay thee with my hands."

Then ran the Knight and clutched the sword and strongly wheeled and threw it; the mystic hand of the Past arose and drew it under in the meer; the King seeing in the eyes of the Knight that the deed was done, and hearing his report of the mystic hand, knew that his time had come, and gave command to the Knight to carry him to the lake, and place him in the barge that plies between the hither and the thither shores of Time.

> "Then loudly cried the bold Sir Bedivere,
> 'Ah! my Lord Arthur, whither shall I go?
> Where shall I hide my forehead and my eyes?
> For now I see the true old times are dead."'
> And slowly answered Arthur from the barge:
> 'The old order changeth, yielding place to new,
> And God fulfils himself in many ways,
> Lest one good custom should corrupt the world!"

That the moral idea is the foundati on of government, is clear, because government implies law, and the essential principle of law is justice. This alone maintains the State, and when its exercise is prevented, either by external force, or internal corruption, the State no longer exists.

From the doctrine that the moral idea is the foundation of the State, flows the necessity of separate governments. The fundamental idea of moral responsibi lity is the same everywhere; but its expression must be modified by time and place. What was right for a man or a State once, may not be right at another time, under other circumstances. It must be modified by place, which is only another name for another condition of things. I need not elaborate: everybody admits that what is right under one condition of things, whether of time or place, may not be right under another.

As to time, the question of expediency may have a large influence. The govern ment may even appear to be inconsistent with itself—declaring war now, for instance, on grounds which would seem insufficient at some other period; but as to the condition of things in different places, the inconsistency of the one organized government must lead to its destruction, or to its injustice. There is no alternative; it must cease, or it must become oppressive. Doubtless there will be many who can see reasons for its perpetuation under such circumstances; but the weaker, or oppressed portion, will be the first to see the matter in a very different light. To them will come, in all its force, the question of dependence or independence, submission or resistance. What does this question imply? Expediency? No: that is the question of policy merely—of policy as to the mode of carrying out the political ends of the State. But the other raises the question of the existence or non-existence of the State. For wherever the question of moral right is raised, justly, by any portion of this world's population, there, I say, it means nothing more nor less than a separate government. This is the issue; and the answer to it is the test of the moral condition of the people. If they make the attempt and fail, whether at Thermopylae or in the shadow of the Carpathians, whether their name be Scot, Pole, Greek, or Hungarian—they become the heroes of history, martyrs, whose blood is the seed of liberty. If they submit, they barter away the last heritage of their claim to the name of man, and consign themselves to the accumulating infamy of years.

Can we say that this issue is not before us? Have we been sincere in believing our social system to be morally right? Have we been walking in craftiness and handling the word of God deceitfully? If so, we are doomed, unless we renounce our error. If not, we are bound to demand for that social system a place of habitation, and a government through which it can be expressed. It cannot be morally expressed under the same government with a people who hold its essential immorality; this drives us to all those shifts of compromise which destroy our honor and sap the foundations of our independence. After having given us this system, and a portion of the earth's surface, and after fully pledging us to the one and the other—to the one by the sacred ties of home, and to the other by the sacred ties of right and duty. Providence permits the issue of moral, intellectual and governmental dependence or independence to come upon us too distinctly for evasion. The federal compact has been broken by the other contracting party, and the man who has been elected President by the Northern States alone, on a sectional issue, feels that he cannot be the President of the South. He dare not claim the right; and the party which elected him claim the position for him as our masters and not as our equals. If we submit, it is but an invitation to an essentially foreign power to take our right of self-government into his hands. It will be the sale of the birth-right, the barter of conscience, and the confession of imbecility. Therefore, the genius of the people is awakening the echoes of the land with her call—

Let a great assembly be
  Of the fearless and the free,
On some spot of Southern ground,
  Where the plains stretch wide around.

Let the blue sky overhead,
  The green earth, on which ye tread,
All that must eternal be,
  Witness the solemnity.

And let Panic, who outspeeds,
  The career of winged steeds
Pass, a disregarded shade,
  Through your phalanx undismayed.

Let a vast assembly be,
  And with great solemnity
Declare, with simple words, that ye
  Are, as God has made you, FREE!

2

www.ingramcontent.com/pod-product-compliance
Lightning Source LLC
LaVergne TN
LVHW020638110826
845149LV00004B/1272

* 9 7 8 1 4 1 8 1 9 0 1 1 8 *